Prolog Programming Success in a Day

By Sam Key

Beginners Guide to Fast, Easy and Efficient Learning of Prolog Programming

2nd Edition

Table of Contents

Introduction

The programing of artificial intelligence and computational linguistics is popular in computer science nowadays. Before, computer programs had a passive character – merely processing data that a user inputs. Nowadays, computers and computer programs are expected to be able to think *on their* own – not just process data, but also to *evaluate* and to make *judgments* and *decisions* about it.

How can a computer program have decision-making skills as efficient as that with living person? Mathematical logic (or formal logic) in computer programming makes this possible. A computer language that makes use of this is Prolog programming, a *logic programming* language.

From the name itself, Prolog programming makes use of formal logic in order to operate commands, variables, and other programming functions. To understand and to write programs in the language of Prolog programming, one has to be oriented with formal logic and learn how to apply this in programming codes according to the syntax specific to Prolog.

This book is a crash course on Prolog programming that will help you learn the essentials of Prolog in a fast, easy, and efficient manner. This book is recommended to programming or computer science beginners who have written computer programs and would like to try incorporating Prolog programming to the practice.

You will find the following lessons and information in this book:

- How Prolog works as a programming language
- Understanding the syntax of terms and clauses in Prolog programming
- Understanding the structure of Prolog programming
- How to write programs and codes using Prolog programming

Prolog Programming Success in a Day 2nd Edition

You will learn the dynamics of Prolog programming by learning how to incorporate formal logic as you write programs and command prompts using this language.

This book will teach you, in very easy and efficient terms, how Prolog programming works and how you can understand and use the language – form clauses, use logical variables, recognize syntax of terms, write programs, among other things that you need to know in order to acquaint yourself with this versatile programming language.

Chapter 1
Prolog as a programming language

Prolog was first conceived in France during the early 1970's. The language was inspired by *logic programming research.*

Logic programming allows the computer program to make logical "decisions" of its own according to terms supplied and programmed by the code writer. The use of formal logic or mathematical logic makes this possible. You will learn how to write codes according to mathematical logic in the later chapters of the book.

Nowadays, Prolog is well-developed as a systematic programming language and is being taught as a core course in computer science classes. If you are going to take a formal course in Prolog and would like to have an advantage, this book will certainly help you learn the essentials of Prolog.

What variables does Prolog use?

Programming languages use *variables* in order to depict an undefined entity or a property. When you want to compute the *truth* or the *validity* of an event, you would normally use variables so that the program can understand *what it is* that you are computing for or evaluating.

In Prolog, you use *logical variables.* This is not the same as the variables being used in other languages. What distinguishes logical variables in Prolog is that the programmer can use it as a "hole" in data structures.

Ordinary variables in other languages have a *fixed* value. The ones in Prolog do not; they change as the computing process occurs. This "hole" is gradually filled as the computation of the program proceeds.

How does computation happen in Prolog?

The basic control flow model – or *algorithm* – used in Prolog is *backtracking.*

Backtracking as an algorithm functions by 1) finding all possible solutions to the computational problem, then 2) re-evaluating each possible solution, then 3) abandons the candidate X (a possible solution) if it finds out that X could not be satisfied according to a valid solution.

A good way to visualize backtracking is finding solutions to a certain problem with constraint. Let's say for example that you intend to enter a private facility that is being guarded by a security force.

First, you think about all the possible ways to enter the facility. Second, you review each manner of entering and *discard* it if the police force would probably catch you while doing the act. This is the algorithm of backtracking in Prolog.

Going back to the example: So how do you realize that the police would most likely catch you in a certain manner of entering the facility?

The answer here is *logic*. This logic is innate in you and you recognize the failure of the situation according to *obvious* logic.

So how do you make a computer program possess this form of logic? You will *encode logic* to the computer program by using *logical variables* in Prolog. Now you understand why the variables in Prolog have to be in a *logical form* (you will learn more about this later). This is so that the variables can become *deciding factors* for the program and come up with a logical conclusion of its own, given data and commands.

What is the form of data in Prolog?

Program clauses and data have the same form in Prolog. Basically, as you will see, entering data in Prolog is always written in the clause form (you will learn how to write this). This is a convenient way to express case analysis (make the program compute cases or occurrences and possibilities).

Take note that this form is *nondeterministic*, meaning that the logical variables that you encode can have "open values" that can be changed or supplemented according to the procedure of the computation. This is why they have been called "holes" in the earlier paragraphs.

As you may now picture in your head, Prolog programs have a relational database that contains *rules* as well as *facts*.

Rules will help the program decide what the logical approach to a computational problem is. It will check against *facts* to see if the plausible solution is acceptable (backtracking). Facts are considered as the "givens" in the code – but take note that facts are always written in as a *logical variable*. Nevertheless, as you will see, there are some control features in Prolog that are being used, yet are not considerably part of "formal logic".

Chapter 2
Understanding Declarative Language

In the previous chapter, you have learned how Prolog works as a logical programming language. The importance and use of logic as an element of the computation process and algorithm has been explained to you. In this chapter, we will look at *clauses* in Prolog. You will also be taught how to read and understand Prolog clauses.

What are clauses in Prolog?

In Prolog programming, clauses are *statements* that provide *information* about what is true about a specific problem (remember that Prolog has a relational database of *rules* and *facts*). These are the "givens" or rather the context of the problem.

In other programming languages, clauses are in the form of *instructions*, not information. These instructions directly tell the program how to accomplish the solution to a problem. As you can see, the program would not think for itself if it merely receives instructions.

In Prolog, however, if you give *information* rather than *instruction*, the program will find its own solutions to the problem.

The clauses in Prolog are *declarative* rather than functional or imperative. Declarative language makes claims and assumes truth or information.

Samples of clauses in Prolog

To make clearer the distinction of declarative language and informational clauses in Prolog, let's compare it with other programming clauses.

In an *imperative language,* you will see the following clause or code:

```
list procedure dog(list a, list
b)
{
   list t = list u = copylist(a);
   while (t.tail != nil) t =
t.tail;
   t.tail = b;
   return u;
}
```

As you can read in the code, this tells the computer to list down the parts and components of the term dog from two separate lists (list A and list A). The computational process *only follows* the command inputted by the programmer.

In a *functional language,* you will see clauses that compare certain terms according to if-and-then statements. The following code makes use of such language:

```
dog(a,b) ≡
 if b = nil then a
else cons(head(a), dog(tail(a),b))
```

In the above code, the program processes information about the term, dog with two components A and B. According to the code, **if** the term does possess not any secondary components (no B characteristics) **then** it will have to redefine the characteristics in A (the code at the last line)

In a *declarative language*, such as in Prolog, we will see an entirely different from and manner of computing information. Look at the following code:

```
dangerous(X) :- sharp_teeth(X).

dangerous(X) :- venomous(X).

guess(X, cat) :- fluffy(X), meows(X), mammal(X).

guess(X, dog) :- fourLegs(X), barks(X).

guess(X, bird) :- withWings(X), hasBeak(X).
```

The clauses that you will find in this code are *informational* and *logical* rather than imperative or functional. The first line of the code is a clause that gives information about the term `dangerous`. If a term has the component `dangerous`, the program would require that it also has the component `sharp_teeth`.

This code, when read as formal logic, would say: *If something is dangerous, then it must have big teeth.* Although it makes use of an if-then sentence, what is being uttered here is not a function, but rather, *information.*

Chapter 3
Complete Syntax of Terms

You now understand the nature of Prolog as a programming language and how it processes information during computation. In this chapter, you will learn about the complete syntax of terms in Prolog so that you can write your own variables and use them in computational operations.

If you were learning a second language, this would be the part where you learn how to write noun phrases, verb phrases, or adjectives – but in this book this will be in the form of programming language. You will learn the different terms in Prolog and how they behave in the program.

What are the terms in Prolog?

Terms are basically the "words" that are being written or coded in programming. If you would like to express an individual, an operation, or a statement, you would need to use terms or combinations of terms in order to do so.

Each programming language has a set of terms, written according to a manner that is acceptable in the language. Prolog has three kinds of terms: *constants, compound terms,* and *variables.* They are very easy to understand and differentiate from one other. They are terms that *stand for* individuals (think of them as noun phrases) but differ in the manner of depicting what they intend to stand for or describe.

Constant

The constant gives a name to an individual that is being depicted in the program. They are the most commonly used terms in programming in order to define elements and individuals. You need constants so you can mention things and identities in the code, just in the same way that you need to identify people's names (or faces) so you can socialize with them.

Constants can either be **atoms** or **numbers**. Prolog actually assumes that an entity is an atom if the string of characters begins with a lowercase letter. Just like the meaning of the word in chemistry, an atom constant describes an action or an entity that could not be changed, reduced, or divided. An atom constant is a term in its simplest terms. Think of a person's surname. This surname could not further be divided into other forms of names.

On the other hand, a **number** is self-explanatory; it defines a fixed quantity or numerical value. It can be a real number or an integer. Be careful because some compound terms make use of *numbers* in the expression. You should be able to identify whether a number is part of a compound term or a constant term. By reading carefully you should be able to internalize this.

In any case, the rules for an atom can be a bit complicated. For instance, an atom can be a quote, word, symbol, or special item. However, a quoted item is only considered an atom if it does not use the single quote (') character. If you wish to include a single quote (') within a quoted atom, you have to duplicate it. When you do, it would appear as: ' ' ' ' .

As for words, they have to begin with a lowercase letter and then followed by a digit, letter, or underscore (_). Symbols, such as -, +, \, /, *, ^, >, <, =, :, ~, . . , ?, #, @, &, *and $* are allowed. Likewise, special items, such as *{ }, [ ], %, ;, and !* are allowed.

Compound Term

These are names for individuals that have parts or could further be "divided" according to each characteristic. Note their distinction from atoms. You can write compound terms in Prolog by using the following forms:

```
happiness(love,euphoria)
novel(anna,Y,50shades)
f(x)
[1, apple, g(f),x]
-(+(15,6), t)
=/= (15+x, (o*d)+66)
```

As you can observe, a compound term is composed of a *functor* (in the first example, the functor is **happiness**) and its *components* (the components of the functor **happiness** are **love** and **euphoria**).

To write a functor with components, simply write the term for the functor. Beside it, place the components written inside a parenthesis. Use commas to separate one component from another. Components may also be comprised of a functor with component (such as in the last line of the above box).

If you are writing the declarative sentence, "*The children of Eve are Cain and Abel*" in Prolog, you can have the following code:

```
eve(cain, abel)
```

IMPORTANT TO REMEMBER: Compound terms can be written with built-in operator declarations. Operator declarations can make the compound term look like an arithmetic problem, but it is not. This is written in such manner so that the form is syntactic and convenient. This does not change the meaning of the compound term; it merely looks like an arithmetic expression.

For example, we have the compound term:

```
=/= (15+x, (o*d)+66)
```

The components of the compound term would be:

Functor: =/=

Components: ($functor_1$) + and ($functor_2$) +

Components of $functor_1$: **15** and **x**

Commponents of $functor_2$: 66 and ($functor_3$) *

Components of $functor_3$: o and d

Do not be confused by operator declarations. Think of them as declarations that separate one component from another and take the function of a functor.

Variable

In Prolog, a variable stands for an individual that could not be predefined or named while the program is still being written. For example, if you are writing a computer program that would calculate your profit, you can first use the variable `gross income` so you that can use a term for identifying what it is that you are computing for.

A variable can practically represent anything. It can represent a name, a number, an array, or a structure. Programs in Prolog work by constraining variables until they acquire specific values, and then they tell you what these values are. For example:

```
y is 2 + 3.
```

Using the example shown above, you will get the following output when you run the code:

```
y = 5
yes.
```

Then again, the program may not constrain the variables to obtain an exact value. Hence, you may get the following:

```
equal ( A, A ) .          % It states that the things are equal to
themselves
y is 2 + 3, equal ( f ( y, z ), w ) .
y = 5
w = f ( 5, _ )
yes
```

Still referring to the example given above, the underscore (_) shows that a variable remains as part of the solution. A result of *yes* may also be obtained if the variables have a value of more than one. This is known as *nondeterminism* and it is allowed. However, if the variables do not have a value that make a solution, a result of *no* is obtained.

List

Every language has to have a method for dealing with object collections. In Prolog, a list is used for this functionality. An example of a list is as follows:

```
[ w, x, y, z ]
```

Brackets are placed at the start and the end while commas are used to separate the elements in a list. The elements are all atoms. A list, however, can have all kinds of elements. These elements can also be in the same list. Take a look at the following example:

```
[ w, W, X, Y, Z ]
[ p ( w, D ), p ( w, D ) ]
[ [ x1, x2, x3 ], [ y1, y2, y3 ], [ z1, z2, z3 ] ]
[ [ X, Y ], [ Y, Z ], quu ( [ x, y, z ], [ x, y, d, i, f ], _ ), k, s, R ]
```

Lists are usually not explicitly defined by most codes, like the ones shown in the example above. Instead, these codes handle lists of various lengths and elements. You can use a bar notation to handle a list without knowing how long it is or what is inside it. For example:

```
[ Head | Tail ]
```

The variable *Head* is a representation of the leftmost element in the list while the variable *Tail* is a representation of the other elements that are also represented as a new list. The head can actually be anything. For instance, it can be a predicate or a new list. However, the tail cannot do the same. It will always remain as the other list.

There are default library rules that are provided such as *reverse*, *length*, and *append*. These rules are easily defined. If you want to know how they work, you can use the following code:

```
? – length ( [ 1, 3, 6 ], What ) .
```

You will get the answer 3.

You can also use the following. Notice the difference between them:

```
? – append ( [ a ], [ b ], z ) .
? – append ( [ a ], b, z ) .
```

Here is another example:

listsplit ([H | T], H, T) .

[H | T] is a list in which *H* is the head while *T* is the tail. If you enter the following query:

```
? – listsplit ( [ v, w, x, y, z ], v, [ w, x, y, z ] ) .
```

you will get the answer *yes*. On the other hand, if you have this query:

```
? – listsplit ( [ v, w, x, y, z ], V, W ) .
```

you will get the answer:

```
V = v
W = [ w, x, y, z ] ;
```

You can even *create* a list such as the following:

```
? – listsplit ( List, v, [ w,  x, y, z ] ) .
List = [ v, w, x, y, z ] ;
```

To help you understand lists further, take a look at the following example of heads and tails. Their results are as follows:

Lists	Heads	Tails
[v, w, x, y, z]	v	[w, x, y, z]
[v]	v	[ ] (a list that is empty)
[[v, w, x], v, w, [v, w]]	[v, w, x]	[v, w, [v, w]]

If you will notice, it is not possible to split up an empty list *[ ]* . Hence, it cannot unify with the [H | T]. If you want to split up lists, you have to use three or more heads, such as the following:

```
[ H1, H2, H3 | Tail ]
```

Referring to the example given above, the list will be split up into its first three elements as well as the rest of it. Nonetheless, you have to remember that it will not succeed if it does not have a sufficient number of elements. In this case, it has to have at least three elements.

Take a look at another sample program. In the following relation, the last element of the list is defined. You can use it as a program to determine the last element in your list.

```
last ( [ Elem ], Elem ) .
last ( [ _ | Tail ], Elem ) : - last ( Tail, Elem ) .
```

```
? – last ( [ a, b, c, d, e ], X ) .
X = e
```

If there is a list that contains a single element, the stop predicate states that that particular element is the last element. Still referring to the example shown above, the last element *Elem* in the list *[_ | Tail]* is the last element of the tail *Tail.* The head in this case is not really necessary, so you can just use an anonymous variable (_) in its place.

The member predicate

Member is one of the standard built-in predicates in Prolog. For example:

```
member ( Element, List ) .
```

Here, *List* can be a representation of any list while *Element* can be a representation of any element. Consider the following example:

```
? – member ( x, [ x, y, z ] ) .
? – member ( y, [ x, y, z ] ) .
? – member ( z, [ x, y, z ] ) .
```

The example shown above succeeds and therefore, returns *yes*.

As for the following query, it returns the succeeding values for Element:

```
? – member ( Element, [ a, b, c ] ) .
```

```
Element = a ;
Element = b ;
Element = c ;
```

The following is how a member predicate is defined:

```
member ( X, [ X | _ ] ) .       % if X = Head, then member ( X, [ Head
                                | Tail ] ) is true
                                 % however, that only applies if X is the
head of                                 the list or if X is a member of
Tail
                                 % example: if member ( X, Tail ) is true.
member ( X, [ _ | Tail ] ) :-  member( X, Tail ) .
```

The append predicate

Append is a built-in predicate that attaches a list at the back of another list. It basically concatenates two different lists. This is how the append predicate is used:

```
append ( As, Bs, Cs )
```

Here, *Cs* is *Bs* appended to *As*.

When using the append predicate to append two lists, you can do it as follows:

```
? – append ( [ u, v, w ], [ x, y, z ], Result ) .
Result = [ u, v, w, x, y, z ]
```

If you want to split a list into two parts, such as the top and the bottom, you can do it as follows:

```
? – append ( ListTop, ListBottom, [ x, y, z ] ) .

ListTop = [ ]
ListBottom = [ x, y, z ] ;

ListTop = [ x ]
ListBottom = [ y, z ] ;

ListTop = [ x, y ]
ListBottom = [ z ] ;

ListTop = [ x, y, z ]
ListBottom = [ ] ;

No
```

If you want to use three variables, you may do so. You can also define the append predicate as follows:

```
append ( [ ], Bs, Bs) .
append ( [ A | As ], Bs, [ A | Cs ] ) : -  append ( As, Bs, Cs ) .
```

As you can see, the first line combines the last couple of lists. Also, it succeeds for queries, such as *append ([ ] , Y, [a])* . and *append ([ ], [a, b, c], [a, b, c])* . . In any case, it binds *Y = [a].*

Still referring to the example shown above, you can see that in the second line, it is stated that the head of A in append (A, B, C) is equivalent to the head of C. Also, appending the tail of A with B will give you the tail of C.

Because Prolog allows nondeterminism, you can use append for various purposes. For instance, you can also use it as a way to implement Last. For example:

```
last ( List, Last ) : - append ( _, [ Last ], List ) .
```

You can also use it for other definitions, such as the following:

```
split ( List, Pivot, Left, Right ) :- append ( Left, [ Pivot | Right ], List ) .
? – split ( [o, o, x, e, e, e ], x, L, R ) .
L = [ o, o ] ,
R = [ e, e, e ] ;
? – split ( A, -, [ o, o ], [ u, u, u ] ) .
A = [ o, o, -, u, u, u ] .
```

Reversing a List

There are a couple of ways on how you can reverse a list. You can either take the head off and append it to the end or take the definition of append and slightly modify it.

The following is an example of the previous:

```
reverse ( [ ], [ ] ) .
reverse ( [ A | As ], BsA : - reverse ( As, Bs ), append ( Bs, [ A ], BsA ) .
```

If you execute this, you have to traverse the list repeatedly. You have to append it every time. Obviously, that can be quite of a hassle. If you do not want to go to all the trouble of doing that, you can use the latter way and slightly modify it:

```
append ( [ ], Bs, Bs ) .
append ( [ A | As ], Bs, [ A | Cs ] ) : - append ( As, Bs, Cs ) .
```

```
revappend ( [ ], Bs, Bs ) .
revappend ( [ A | As ], Bs, Cs ) : - revappend ( As, [ A | Bs ], Cs ) .
```

```
reverse ( As, Bs ) : - revappend ( As, [ ], Bs ) .
```

This way of reversing a list is much more efficient. The strategy used for revappending is referred to as the accumulating parameter.

Chapter 4
Structures of Programs

You have now learned about terms in Prolog and how to write them in proper syntax. In this chapter, you will learn about the *structure* of programs in Prolog so you can get started to actual programming. We will talk about coding structure in this chapter.

Things to remember about programming in Prolog

Programs in Prolog consist of *procedures*. A procedure has to be a "complete thought" about term and what are the truths and rules about that term. Think of this as similar to a paragraph with a concise explanation about a subject.

Procedures consist of *clauses*. In general programming, a clause comprises a single line in a code and it contains information about terms, variables, or compound terms.

A clause can have different forms according to what you need it to mean. Think of this as sentences with various forms and function.

The distinctive thing about Prolog is that each clause is a *fact* or a *rule* (remember the relational database of database of Prolog). Clauses are written in a form that utilizes formal, mathematical logic. You don't have to master all argument forms in mathematical logic; knowing basic logical rules (such as derivational relationships and if-then statements) is enough. This is what you will use in Prolog codes, by the way, as you will see later.

In Prolog, programs are executed by *posing queries*. We'll get back to this later. As of now, let's talk about procedures and their structure.

Here is an example of a procedure that would make you understand Prolog structure more efficiently:

```
dogRetreiver(sam).
dogRetriever(lucy).
dogRetriever(X) :- golden(X), mammal(X), hasFur(X), obedient(X).
```

The entire code in the box is a *procedure* for `dogRetriever`.

`dogRetriever` is what we call the *predicate* of the procedure. Think of this as the topic of the code or the procedure. We are talking about properties and components for `dogRetriever` here.

Each line in the code is a *clause*. Not all clauses are the same. You have learned that clauses can either be *rules* or *facts*.

The first two clauses – `dogRetriever(sam)` and `dogRetriever(lucy)`- are two clauses that determine *fact*. In these two clauses, we state that `sam` and `lucy` are components of the predicate `dogRetriever`. This is a fact. You may wish to add more components of the predicate by writing more factual clauses.

The last line is a *rule*. Take note of how it is written and what are the operational symbols included in it. The last line as a clause basically reads as:

If any component X is a component of the functor `dogRetriever`, then the component X must also be a component of the functors `golden`, `mammal`, `obedient`, and `hasFur`.

Easy and simple to read, isn't it?

How is formal logic used in the structure of the code?

We have been discussing for the most part that Prolog is *logic programming*. We program logic so that the software can make logical conclusions of its own. This is the part where you will see this *fleshed out* in the code.

Take note of the *nature* and *structure* of the rule clause. This is an "if-then" clause (not to be confused in functional programming). "If-then" arguments, in formal logic, are used to describe relationships between statements. The second statement assumes truth if the first statement is true.

In formal logic, this is written as:

p > q

If *p*, then *q*.

The following arguments have the same logical form:

- If I am going to Spain, I need a passport, ticket, and luggage.

Are you truly going to Spain? Then you need a passport, ticket, and luggage.

- If I am going to write, I need writing tools.

Are you going to write? Then you need writing tools.

Let's translate the first argument as if it were a Prolog code:

```
travelSpain(X) :- passport(X), ticket(X), luggage(X).
```

In this rule clause, if you are a component of `travelSpain,` then you also have to be a component of `passport,` `ticket,` and `luggage.`

Take note that we *do not read* the programming code as if it were an argument with formal logic. This code actually reads as:

X is a component of `travelSpain` if X is a component of `passport`, `ticket`, and `luggage`.

The way of reading code – as a logical statement – is contrary to reading logical statements. In the first place, we eliminate the "then" in the code. We only have "if's" in Prolog programming.

If this sounds confusing, in the next chapter we will talk more about understanding clauses. We just stressed in this part how logic is applied in Prolog.

Queries, replies and program execution

Now let's talk about *queries*. We have mentioned earlier that a Prolog program is executed by posing queries.

This is an example of a Prolog code that poses queries (based on our procedure for `dog`:

```
?- dog(sam).
yes
?- dog(adam).
no
```

Codes that start with `?` are called queries. `yes` and `no` in the code are called *replies*. The replies are given to you by the program.

As you can observe, replies are based on the facts that are specified in the code.

Since `sam` is a component of `dog` in the code, the program will give a reply of **`yes`**. Since `jane` has not been specified as a component of `dog`, the reply will be no.

In the next chapter, we will have an in-depth discussion about clauses, their structures and parts, and how we interpret them.

Chapter 5
Understanding and Interpreting Clauses

Clauses are very important in Prolog. You need to understand how they work and how you can write them properly according to what you mean. They make up the entire program code.

Let's look at the structure of the *clause* itself:

```
Head :- Body.

Head.
```

Take note of the operational symbol used (**:-**) – the colon with a hyphen. This reads "if", "provided that", or "turnstile".

The *head* is the first half of a rule clause, preceded by :-. What proceeds after :- ia the *body* . Take note of the full stop at the end.

A head composes a fact clause, while an head and body comprises a rule clause.

Look at the following code:

```
woman(jane).
woman(pretty).
woman(nice).

woman(X):- lovely(X), wearsMakeup(X), wearsDress(X), wife(X)
```

In the code, we have given the factual components of the functor `woman`. We have also mentioned in the rule clause that X is a component of `woman` if X is a component of `lovely`, `wearsMakeup`, `wearsDress`, and `wife`.

If we look at the procedure as part of a program that makes assertions about women, then we are looking at a program that thinks women are always named Jane, are pretty, and are nice in nature. If the program encounters a person, this person will be considered as a woman by the program if the person is lovely, wears make-up, a dress, and is also a wife.

Here you can see how artificial intelligence works and how logic is used in order to make the artificial intelligence possible. Basically, the program is artificially intelligent enough to recognize a person as a woman upon encounter. However, if we look at the code, the understanding of the artificial intelligence is pretty insufficient. We have merely created an artificially intelligent program that has a *stereotypical* or even misogynistic view about women. Be responsible about the codes and artificial intelligence that you program! Women don't have to wear make-up before they become women!

Clauses and goals

Let's go back to understanding Prolog. Instead of looking at clauses as logical assertions (which is the conceptual side) let's look at it in the programmer's lens.

Basically, the body of a rule clause contains *goals*. In programming, goals are defined as values that would satisfy the head of a clause.

Look at the following explanation and labels:

```
loves(potatoes, facebook, X)   :-   girl(X), straight(X), cute(X)
```

The code in this box is the head

The code in this box is the body *and contains* goals. *The goals are the* functors *in the term.*

Let's assume that the codes in the boxes comprise a single rule clause. This code talks about what a particular guy loves – potatoes, facebook, and *something else*. How do we know if this object could earn the heart of the man, in the way that potatoes and facebook does?

It has to fulfill the *goals* of the body. X should be a girl, straight, and cute. The X that we are trying to qualify in the body is actually a *girlfriend*.

Interpretation of clauses

Clauses in Prolog can be given a *declarative* reading or a *procedural* reading. This depends on what you intend your program to do or to achieve – the purpose of what you are coding. Nevertheless, before we get to actual program writing, let's try to read a clause in two ways.

For example, we have the following clause:

```
A :- B1, B2, B3, B4,… Bn.
```

If we look at it in a *declarative reading,* this clause would read:

"That A is attestable follows from goals B_1, B_2, B_3, B_4... B_n being attestable."

As you can observe, the sentence is declarative.

On the other hand, in a *procedural reading,* the clause would read:

"To execute procedure A, the procedures called by goals B_1, B_2, B_3, B_4... B_n are executed first."

What you are performing in the Prolog code is not a "procedure" per se.

Remember that Prolog utilizes declarative language, not a *functional* one. The closest thing that it can have with functional languages is the element of a procedural command. We do not even have procedural commands in Prolog; what we only have here are *restrictions* for what can be executed as procedures.

Let's go back to our example in the first chapter about the challenge of entering a private facility guarded by security officers. If you give this challenge to a Prolog program, it will look at all the possible ways to enter the building. Then, through the algorithm of backtracking, it will eliminate options that are rendered unfeasible or impossible (if you don't wish to get caught by the security officers).

We have asked *how* the program can have a certain logical thinking that is comparable to a human being who knows what is safe and unsafe. This question is being answered now, if you understand clearly how clauses are interpreted in Prolog.

A Prolog program will have this flow of thinking:

"Think about all the ways to enter the building. *Check*. Let's look at option A. What are the goals involved in option A? Are these goals attestable? *Counterchecks option A against facts and other rules in the program. Finds out that it does not satisfy one goal. Discards.* Looks at option B...Repeats the process."

How does the program exactly "countercheck"? It looks at the goals in the rule clause if they are provable (this is for a declarative reading).

When it has found the solution to the problem – the way to enter the building – it would execute first the goals in the body (procedures B_1, B_2, B_3, B_4... B_n, for example) that would allow the execution of the head (procedure A).

Let's assume that you have written the code for the Prolog program that will find solutions to enter a building, given certain constraints.

You can execute the program through posing *queries*:

```
?- entry(throughCar).

no

?- entry(byWalking).

no

?- entry(byInvisibilityCloak).

yes
```

Before the program gives an answer to the query, it has to check first whether the given term is *executable* by executing goals that are associated with the term. This happens in a procedural reading. In a declarative reading, there is an evaluation of whether terms are provable or attestable.

As you can see, you would need to code constraints, rules, and facts, so that the artificial intelligence can evaluate queries according to constraints and procedures. You will learn this in the last chapter, coding programs. But before we get to that, we have an important rule to understand about clauses: *unification*.

What is unification?

Remember that in case substitutions can be made for any variables in the two terms then the two terms are said to unify. The aforementioned terms will then be made identical in a sense. However, if there can be no substitution, then the two terms could not be unified.

This is expressed in the Unification Algorithm:

- Constants will always unify if these constants are identical
- Variables will always unify with any type of term, that includes other variables as well
- Compound terms will definitely unify only if their functors as well as their components unify

To further illustrate this, let's look at the following terms:

```
f(X, a(b,c))
```

Unifies with

```
f(d, a(Z,c))
```

The two terms are made equal if `d` is substituted for `X`, and `b` is substituted for `Z`. This is possible because `X` and `d` are both variables. `b` is substituted for `Z` because their functors unify.

What terms could not be unified? Look at the next two terms:

```
f(c, a(b,c))
```

Does not unify with

```
f(Z, a(Z,c))
```

You cannot substitute terms for variables.

Chapter 6
Sample Prolog Program Code

You have now learned how Prolog works as a logic programming language. You have been taught how to write clauses, understand them, and how you can work together facts and rules into a single code for a procedure.

Let's see how far you have learned the lessons in the previous chapters. Here is how a Prolog program code looks like:

```
/* At the Cafe */

waitress(anna).
waitress(therese).

customer(evan).
customer(thomas).

generous(X) :- fat_purse(X).
generous(X) :- gives_tip(X).

guest(X, miss) :- young(X), pretty(X), lady(X).
guest(X, mister) :- rich(X), oldMan(X).
guest(X, parent) :- withKids(X), hasBag(X).
```

This code is a program about the café. The artificially intelligent program knows details about people, guests, and the staff.

From what you can read in the code above, this is what the program knows:

There are two waitresses who work in the café, and their names are Anna and Therese.

There are two customers at the café: Evan and Thomas.

The program also knows that someone is generous if they have a fat purse and gives tips.

The program will identify guests. The guest is a miss if the person is young, pretty, and is a lady.

It is a master if the person is rich and is an old man.

Lastly, the guest is a parent if the person has kids and has a bag.

You can ask the program to evaluate persons according to their characteristics.

Let's say that the program is installed to an AI robot that identifies guests who enter the café and reports to the manager, who studies the demographic of people who enter the café.

People enter the café. Let's say that there are two guests who enter. The robot has a camera that recognizes characteristics and groups people according to certain traits. Let's add some the robot's observations (in code form) to the code for the café:

```
rich(john).
rich(maxwell).
rich(thomas).

withKids(MrBrown).
withKids(amy).
withKids(stacey).
withKids(lucas).

hasBag(lucas)
hasBag(emma)
hasBag(Janine)

fat_purse(stacey)

lady(emma).
lady(janine).
lady(stacey).
lady(anna).

pretty(emma).

young(emma).
young(lucas).
```

Let's now imagine the program being executed. Here are the following queries and replies that can be made about some guests:

```
?- guest(emma, miss)
yes
?- guest(lucas, parent)
yes
?- guest(lucas, generous)
no
```

From what you have learned in this book, you should understand how the program was able to determine whether a guest was a parent or a miss, or whether they are generous or not. Most of all, you should understand how the program can use *backtracking* in order to check all possible categories for the customers and abandon the choices that does not fit them.

Chapter 7
Arguments

Facts with Arguments

Complicated facts consist of relations and items, known as arguments, to which they refer. It is possible for facts to have an arbitrary number of arguments starting from zero onwards. An example of a general model is as follows:

```
relation ( < argument1 > , < argument2 > , . . . . . , < argument > ) .
```

Take note that relation names have to start with a lowercase letter. For example:

```
likes ( mary, john) .
```

Using the example shown above, you can say that there is a relationship between *mary* and *john*, and this relationship is connected via *likes*. You may read it as *mary likes john* or *john likes mary*.

As a programmer, you may find this reversibility to be highly useful. Then again, it can also be detrimental in the sense that your viewers may not immediately understand what you mean.

Thus, you must always be consistent and clear on *how* you want your viewers to interpret and understand the relation that you show them. Likewise, you have to be consistent and clear on *when* you want them to interpret such relation.

Furthermore, you have to remember the names of the relations that you defined. Keep in mind that the system is only aware of the relations that you define, with the exception of several relations that it has built into it.

Take a look at the following examples of facts with arguments. It is a sample database that tells you who eats what in a certain world model.

eats (james, peaches) .	/* "James eats peaches" */
eats (james, porterhouse_steaks) .	/* "James eats porterhouse steaks" */
eats (jack, lemons) .	/* "Jack eats lemons" */
eats (sue, grapes) .	/* "Sue eats grapes" */
eats (sue, cakes) .	/* "Sue eats cakes" */

So if you are asked certain questions, you can get the following interactions:

? – eats (james, peaches) .	/* does this have a match in your database? */
yes	/* yes, it matches the first clause in the database */
? – eats (sue, grapes) .	/* do you have a fact that states sue eats grapes? */
yes	/* yes you do, it is in the fourth clause in the database */
? – eats (wendy, kiwis) .	/* does this query match a clause in the database? */
no	/* no, it does not match a clause based on the above given database */
? – eats (james, bananas) .	/* does james eat bananas? */
no	/* no, the database does not say whether or not james eats bananas */

Consider the following database. In this next example, the predicate *age* is used to state the ages of different people:

```
age ( liz, 40 ) .                /* Liz is 40 years old */
age ( jack, 50 ) .               /* Jack is 50 years old */
age ( kenneth, 70 ) .            /* Kenneth is 70 years old */
age ( jenna, 39 ) .              /* Jenna is 39 years old */
age ( tracey, 45 ) .             /* Tracey is 45 years old */
```

Still referring to example give above, you can get the following interactions when asked certain questions:

```
? – age ( jenna, 39 ) .          /* Is Jenna 39 years old? */
yes                              /* Yes, she is according to the fourth clause in the database */
? – ( jack, 50 ) .               /* For whatever relation, is Jack 50? */
no                               /* You get no because age is the only relation stated in the database */
                                 /* The query is not successful because it does not match any clause in the database */
? – age ( kenneth, seventy ) .   /* Is Kenneth seventy years old? */
no                               /* No, because seventy and 70 are two different entities */
                                 /* The query does not match any clause in the database */
```

Chapter 8
Argument Passing and Control

When Prolog comes across a foreign predicate during run time, it calls a function that is specified in this foreign predicate's predicate definition. The arguments *1, < arity >,* and . . . pass the arguments to the goal as terms. You have to declare foreign functions as type *foreign_t*. Keep in mind that deterministic foreign functions can return control to Prolog using two alternatives. These are the following:

(return) foreign_t PL fail ( )

Fail and begin backtracking. PL_fail is defined as return FALSE.

(return) foreign_t PL succeed ( )

Succeed deterministically. PL_succeed is defined as return TRUE.

Non-Deterministic Foreign Predicates

Foreign predicates are actually deterministic by default. You can register predicates as non-deterministic predicates if you use the *PL_FA_NONDETERMINISTIC* attribute. You may find that it is quite more difficult and complicated to write non-deterministic foreign predicates. This is because the foreign function has to obtain context information in order to generate a new solution. Take note that this foreign function has to be prepared in order for it to be simultaneously active in more than a single goal.

Take a look at the following example. In this sample predicate, the natural_number_below_n/2 is a non-deterministic foreign predicate. It backtracks over the natural numbers that are lower than the initial argument.

```
quotient_below_n ( Q, N ) : -
        natural_number_below_n ( N, N1 ) ,
        natural_number_below_n ( N, N2 ) ,
```

```
Q = : N1 / N2 , ! .
```

Still referring to the example shown above, the function *natural_number_below_n/2* generates solutions for its invocations simultaneously.

In Prolog, the non-deterministic foreign functions always have to be prepared to deal with three different calls.

1. *Initial call (PL_FIRST_CALL)*

A frame has just been created for the foreign function. Prolog asks it to give the first answer.

2. *Redo call (PL_REDO)*

According to the foreign function's previous invocation, backtracking is possible. This foreign function is related to the present goal and has to produce a new solution.

3. *Terminate call (PL_PRUNED)*

A cut has destroyed the choice point that the foreign function left. This foreign function is offered the chance to clean its environment.

The type of call and the context information are given by the argument of type *control_t*, which is appended to the argument list for deterministic foreign functions. The type of call is extracted by the macro *PL_foreign_control ( )* from the control argument. A context handle can be passed by the foreign function with the use of *PL_retry* ( )* macros. Likewise, the foreign function can extract the handle from the extra argument with the use of the *PL_foreign_context* ( )* macro.

```
( return ) foreign_t PL_retry_address ( void * )
```

Defined as return_PL_retry_address (n). As PL_retry ( ), it ensures that an address returned by malloc ( ) is recovered properly by PL_foreign_context_address ( ) .

(return) foreign_t PL_retry (intptr_t value)

Foreign functions succeed as they leave a choice point. They are called once more when backtracking is done. The control argument, however, says that it is a 'redo' call. So, the macro PL_foreign_context ( ) returns the handle passed through PL_retry ( ). Such handle is a signed value that is a couple of bits smaller than the pointer.

int PL_foreign_control (control_t)

It extracts a call type from the control argument. Take note that it is necessary for the function to be prepared in order to deal with the PL_PRUNED case. It also has to be aware that other arguments are invalid.

intptr_t PL_foreign_context (control_t)

It extracts the context from the context argument. The value of the context is 0L if PL_FIRST_CALL is the type of call. Otherwise, the value is the one returned by the last PL_retry ( ) that is associated with it.

predicate_t PL_foreign_context_predicate (control_t)

It fetches the predicate that executes the function. The returned predicate, however, does not refer to the predicate that is imported. Instead, it refers to the final definition. If a non-deterministic foreign function returns through PL_fail ( ) or PL_succeed ( ), it is assumed that the foreign function has cleared the environment. Thus, a call with the control argument PL_PRUNED does not follow.

void * PL_foreign_context_address (control_t)

It extracts the address that is passed by PL_retry_address ( ).

If you want to know how a non-deterministic foreign predicate definition looks like, consider the following code:

```
typedef struct              /* It defines a context structure */

{...
} context;

foreign_t
my_function( term_t a0, term_t a1, control_t handle )
{ struct context * ctxt;

  switch( PL_foreign_control ( handle ) )
  { case PL_FIRST_CALL :
      ctxt = malloc ( sizeof ( struct context ) );
      ...
      PL_retry_address ( ctxt );
    case PL_REDO :
      ctxt = PL_foreign_context_address ( handle );
      ...
      PL_retry_address ( ctxt );
    case PL_PRUNED:
      ctxt = PL_foreign_context_address ( handle );
      ...
      free( ctxt );
      PL_succeed;
  }
}
```

Chapter 9
Atoms and Functors

You learned in Chapter 3 what atoms and functors are. The following are functions that use atoms and functors to communicate:

atom_t PL_new_atom (const char *)

It returns the atom handle for any given C string, and it succeeds at all times. The returned handle stays valid until the atom is no longer referenced.

The following atoms are provided as macros and provide access to the list constructor's name and the empty list symbol.

atom_t ATOM_nil (ATOM_nil)

It is an atomic constant that represents an empty list. Whenever possible, you should use PL_unify_nil ( ) , PL_get_nil ( ) , or PL_put_nil ( ).

atom_t ATOM_dot (ATOM_dot)

It is an atomic constant that represents the list constructor's name. The list constructor is actually created with the use of PL_new_functor (ATOM_dot, 2). Whenever possible, you should use PL_unify_list ( ), PL_get_list ( ), or PL_put_list ( ).

const char * PL_atom_chars (atom_t atom)

It returns the C string for the text that is represented by the atom. Prolog does not change the returned text. It is also not possible to modify the existing content, including *temporary* content because the string might be in read-only memory. If the atom is garbage collected, the returned string is not valid.

functor_t PL_new_functor (atom_t name, int arity)

It returns the function identifier, which is a handle for the name or arity pair. For the whole session, the returned handle stays valid.

int PL_functor_arity (functor_t f)

It returns the arity of the functor.

atom_t PL_functor_name (functor_t f)

It returns the atom that represents the name of the functor.

Atoms and Atom Garbage Collection

Due to the introduction of atom garbage collection, the atoms do not live as long as the process anymore. Their life span has become just as long as they are referenced. For instance, atom garbage collections in the single-threaded version are invoked at the call-port alone. With the exception of the invoking thread, they also appear asynchronously in the multithreaded version.

There are two added functions in Prolog, which are meant to deal with these atom garbage collections. They are the following:

void PL_unregister_atom (atom_t atom)

It decrements the atom's reference count. It raises an assertion error when the reference count goes lower than zero.

void PL_register_atom (atom_t atom)

It increments the atom's reference count by one. The atom is automatically returned with at least one reference count by PL_new_atom ( ).

When it comes to atom garbage collection, the following calls are not the same:

```
PL_unify_atom_chars ( t, “text” ) ;
PL_unify_atom ( t, PL_new_atom ( “text” ) ) ;
```

The atom *text*'s reference count is incremented by the latter. This ensures that the atom is never collected. Ideally, you should use the functions **_nchars* ( ) or **_chars* whenever possible.

Chapter 10
Recursion

In Prolog, recursion is the process that performs a certain operation repeatedly. It does this either over an entire data structure or until it reaches a certain point. During recursion, the program calls itself until it reaches the final point. As the programmer, you have the first fact that serves as the stopping condition, which is followed by a rule or set of rules that performs another operation before it reinvokes itself.

To help you understand the concept of recursion further, consider the following example:

```
on_route ( rome ) .

on_route ( Place ) : -
      move ( Place, Method, NewPlace ) ,
      onroute ( NewPlace ) .

move ( home, taxi, halifax ) .
move ( halifax, train, gatwick ) .
move ( gatwick, plane, rome ) .
```

As you can see in the example shown above, on_route is a recursive predicate. The program checks if you can travel from a certain place towards the place rome. The first clause checks if you have already arrived at that place. If you have, the program stops. On the other hand, the second clause checks if you have moved from your current place to another place. A database of your possible moves is displayed at the right. The recursive, then, checks if NewPlace is on_route to rome.

How about if you pose the query ? – on_route (home) . ? Well, this will match the second clause. It will not match the first clause because rome and home do not unify. There are a couple of subgoals that make up the second clause. The first asks you if you can move from home to a new location. For example:

```
move ( home, Method, NewPlace ) .
```

```
Method = taxi, NewPlace = Halifax
```

You will get the result *yes* because it is possible to move from home to Halifax via a taxi. Then, you can recursively see if you can find a route to rome from halifax by repeating the same process. You can do this when you execute the new *subgoal on_route (halifax)* .

How to Write Recursive Procedures

When you write a recursive procedure, you have to remember that there will always be at least one rule for the recursive case and at least one rule for the base case.

The Base Case

Usually, the rules for the base case are related to dealing with the simplest example of the problem you are attempting to solve. For instance, you may have a single member or a list without any members. If you are handling a tree structure, your base case may deal with a tree with only one node or a tree that is empty.

The Recursive Case

When it comes to rules for the recursive case, you have to ponder how you can solve your present problem, assuming that you have already solved similar yet smaller problems before. For instance, if you are supposed to add a list of ten numbers, consider if you can add the last nine numbers and add their total to the first. A lot of programmers think that it is much easier and convenient to add the first nine numbers first and then add their total to the last number. However, in Prolog, it is actually easier to deal with the first item in a list instead of the last. So in this, you are better off adding the last nine numbers first.

To help you understand the concepts of the base case and the recursive case better, take a look at the following examples:

Adding Numbers In a List

```
% addup (List, Sum )
% It binds Sum to the sum of the numbers in the list.
% It assumes that every member of the list is actually a number.
% The List has to be instantiated when addup is called.
% For example:
% ? – addup ( [ 1, 2, 3, 4 ],  X ) .
% X = 10

%% base case
addup ( [ ], 0 ) .
% The sum of the numbers in the empty list is zero

%% recursive case : in case the rule for the base case does not match,
you have to do this:
addup ( [ FirstNumber | RestOfList ], Total ) : - addup ( RestOfList,
TotalOfRest),

% It adds the numbers in RestOfList

Total is FirstNumber + TotalOfRest.
```

Referring to the example given above, *addup (RestOfList, TotalOfRest)* is the recursive call. It adds up everything in the list, with the exception of the first item. Then, it binds their sum to *TotalofRest*. Finally, the line that follows your recursive call binds *Total* to the sum of *TotalOfRest* and *FirstNumber*.

Determining the Last Item In a List

```
% lastitem ( List,  Last )
% It binds Last to the item at the end of List.
% List has to be instantiated during the time of call. It should also
contain at least one item.
% For example:
% ? – lastitem ( [ a, b, c, d ] , X ) .
% X = d
```

```
%% base case : a list with a single item.
lastitem ( [ OnlyOne ] , OnlyOne ) .

%% recursive case: it ignores the first item and searches for the last
item from the rest of the list
lastitem ( [ First | Rest ] , Last ) : - lastitem ( Rest, Last ) .
```

Referring to the example shown above, List has to have at least one item. It is not allowed to be empty.

Chapter 11
Built-In Goals

In Chapter 5, you have read about goals, although not fully elaborated. In this chapter, the built-in goals in Prolog will be discussed.

Utility Goals

- halt – It stops Prolog and resumes the operating system.
- help (S) – S represents an atom. For example:

```
help ( assert )
```

- trace – It turns on trace.
- notrace – It turns off trace.

Universals

- fail – It always fails as a goal.
- true – It always succeeds as a goal.

Loading Programs

The standard predicates for loading programs in Prolog are the *bracket loader notation [. . .], consult*, and *reconsult.*

- [. . .] – The bracket notation means that you have to consult the item at the beginning of the list first, and then move on to the second item, and then to the next, and so on. For example:

```
[ F1, F2, . . . ]
```

Here, the program consults F1 first and then F2, and so on and so forth.

- consult (F) – It loads the program from the file F. Take note that F has to be bound to the file designator expression. Make sure that you consider your file system.

  For example:

  ```
  F = ' [ root.programs.prolog ] prog.pro '
  ```

  You can also write:

  ```
  F = ' / home/ user/ prolog/ sample.p1 '
  ```

- reconsult (F) – It is similar to consult, with the exception of their predicate. With reconsult, the definition of every predicate that has already been defined is replaced with a new definition that is being loaded.

Arithmetic Goals

They test what they appear to test. For example:

```
A > B , A < B , A =< B , A >= B
```

Using the example shown above, *A* and *B* have to be bound to numbers so they can either fail or succeed. Otherwise, it will not be possible to test them and an error will occur.

Testing Types

- integer (x) – It tests if x is bound to a particular integer.
- string (x) – It tests if x is bound to a particular string.
- real (x) – It tests if x is bound to a particular real number.
- atom (x) – It tests if x is bound to a symbolic atom. The following are examples of an atom:

  ```
  ? – atom ( foot ) .
  yes
  ? – atom ( "foot" ) .
  no
  ```

```
? – atom ( 'foot' ) .
yes
? – atom ( 3 ) .
no
```

Equality of Expressions

Consider the following examples:

```
A = B , A \= B
```

```
? – [ A, B | R ] = [ x, y, z ] .
A = x, B = y, R = [ z ]
? – [ A, B, C ] = [ x, y ] .
no
```

They test whether or not A and B can be unified.

```
A == B , A \== B
```

```
? – A = 3, B = 1 * 3, A == B .
no
? – A = x, [ B | _ ] = [ x, y, z ], A == B .
A = x, B = x
```

They test whether or not A and B are co-bound. For instance, they test whether or not A and B share the same value or have been bound to the same value.

Control

- call (P) – It forces P to become a goal. It succeeds if P does become a goal. Otherwise, it fails.
- ! – It is the cut predicate. It eliminates the choices in a derivation tree.

Testing for Variables

- var (X) – It tests whether or not X is bound to a variable.
- ground (G) – It tests whether or not G has unbound logical variables.

Assert and Retract

- assert (C), assertz (C) – It asserts the clause C into the database below the other clauses with a similar key predicate.
- asserta (C) – It asserts the clause C into the database above the other clauses with a similar key predicate. The first predicate that the clause encounters when it is read from left to right is its key predicate.
- retract (C) – It retracts C from the database. It has to be instantiated enough in order to identify the predicate key.

Binding Logical Variables to Numeric Values

For example:

```
A is Z
```

The logical variable is bound to the numerical value of Z. The expression Z has to either be a number-valued expression or a number. It also has to be parenthesized conventionally.

Negation As Failure

The negation-as-failure *not* predicate can be defined as:

```
not ( P ) : - call ( P ) , ! , fail .
not ( P ) .
```

Input/Output

- read (Y) – It reads the Prolog type expression from the current port and then stores the value in Y.
- write (Z) – It writes the Prolog expression that is bound to Z into the current output port.
- see (Y) – It opens the port for the input file bound to Y. Then, the subsequent input for *read* is taken from such port.
- seeing (Y) – It succeeds if Y is bound to the current read port.
- seen – It closes the selected input file or port and makes *read* look at the user.
- tell (Y) – It opens the port for the output file that is bound to Y. Then, the subsequent output from *display* or *write* is sent to such port.
- telling (Y) – It succeeds if Y is bound to the current output port.
- told – It closes the selected output file or port and then reverts to the screen output.
- tab (N) – It writes N spaces to the selected output port.
- nl – It means next line.

Terms and Clauses as Data

- arg (A, B, C) – *A* represents a whole number while *B* has to be bound to a functor expression and *C* has to be bound to *B*'s Nth argument.
- functor (A, B, C) – *A* has to be bound to a functor expression of *b (. . .). B* has to be bound to *b* while *C* has to be bound to *B*'s argument amount.
- clause (Y, Z) – It retrieves the memory's clauses whose body matches *Z* and head matches *Y. Y* has to be instantiated enough in order to identify its head's main predicate.
- name (A, L) – It converts between the atom and the list.

Chapter 12
Arithmetic Operators

If you are planning to carry out complex mathematical computations, Prolog is not an ideal programming language to use. Nevertheless, it still does have some arithmetic capabilities.

Arithmetic and Bitwise Functors

- **(* *)** – Power
- **sin** – Sine
- **cos** – Cosine
- **atan** – Arc tangent
- **exp** – Exponentiation
- **log** – Log
- **sqrt** – Square root
- **(> >)** – Bitwise right shift
- **(< <)** – Bitwise left shift
- **(^)** – Bitwise and
- **(ˇ)** – Bitwise or
- \ – Bitwise complement

Consider the following:

- **A + B** is the sum of A and B
- **A – B** is the difference of A and B
- **A * B** is the product of A and B

- **A / B** is the quotient of A and B
- **A ^ B** is A to the power of B
- **-A** is the negative of A
- **abs (A)** is the absolute value of A
- **sin (A)** is the sine of A degrees
- **cos (A)** is the cosine of A degrees
- **max (A, B)** is the larger of A and B
- **sqrt (A)** is the square root of A
- < < > > is left and right shift

Relational Operators

=:= equal

=\= not equal

> greater than

>= greater than or equal to

< less than

=< less than or equal to

=, ==, and =:=

• = is the unification predicate. It succeeds if it is able to unify its arguments. Otherwise it fails.

• \= is the negation of the unification predicate. It succeeds if = fails, and vice-versa.

• == is the identity predicate. It succeeds if its arguments are identical. Otherwise, it fails.

• \== is the negation of the identity predicate. It succeeds if == fails, and vice-versa.

• =:= is the arithmetic equality predicate. It succeeds if its arguments evaluate to the same integer.

• =\= is the arithmetic inequality predicate. It succeeds if its arguments evaluate to different integers.

Precedence of Operators

If there is more than one operator in an arithmetic expression, the rules regarding the precedence of operators should be followed.

The operators that have a higher precedence are * and /, and should therefore be read before + and -.

Operators that have the same precedence are read from left to right.

So **A + B * C – D** is read as **A + (B * C) – D** .

Conclusion

Thank you again for purchasing this book!

I hope this book was able to help you to learn about Prolog programming.

The next step is to write complicated codes and script your programs!

Finally, if you enjoyed this book, please take the time to share your thoughts and post a review on Amazon. It'd be greatly appreciated!

Finally, if you enjoyed this book, please take the time to share your thoughts and post a review on Amazon. We do our best to reach out to readers and provide the best value we can. Your positive review will help us achieve that. It'd be greatly appreciated!

Thank you and good luck!

Check Out My Other Books

Below you'll find some of my other popular books that are popular on Amazon and Kindle as well. Simply click on the links below to check them out. Alternatively, you can visit my author page on Amazon to see other work done by me.

Android Programming in a Day

Python Programming in a Day

C Programming Success in a Day

C Programming Professional Made Easy

JavaScript Programming Made Easy

PHP Programming Professional Made Easy

C ++ Programming Success in a Day

Windows 8 Tips for Beginners

HTML Professional Programming Made Easy

If the links do not work, for whatever reason, you can simply search for these titles on the Amazon website to find them.

www.ingramcontent.com/pod-product-compliance
Lightning Source LLC
Chambersburg PA
CBHW070959180526
45168CB00003B/1216

* 9 7 8 1 5 1 6 8 7 8 4 4 4 *